Love And Smiles

JERRY DODGION

Recorded by JERRY DODGION
on THE JOY OF SAX

Love And Smiles Music (LSM 101)

JERRY DODGION, alto sax
BRAD LEALI, alto sax
FRANK WESS, tenor sax
DAN BLOCK, tenor sax
JAY BRANDFORD, baritone sax
MIKE LeDONNE, piano
DENNIS IRWIN, bass
JOE FARNSWORTH, drums

Recorded October 2, 2003

CD available at www.JerryDodgion.com

INSTRUMENTATION
1st part: **Alto Sax 1**
2nd part: **Alto Sax 2**
3rd part: **Tenor Sax 1**
4th part: **Tenor Sax 2**
5th part: **Baritone Sax**
Rhythm Section: **Piano, Bass, Drums**
FULL SCORE

A DON SICKLER PRODUCTION
SECOND FLOOR MUSIC

HL00000996

Recorded on THE JOY OF SAX / Jerry Dodgion (Love and Smiles Music LSM 101)

Love And Smiles

JERRY DODGION

engraved by Osho Endo

Love and Smiles

E
Alt 1
Alt 2
Ten 1
Ten 2
Bari
Bass
Dr
27
F
Alt 1
mf
cresc.
decresc.
Alt 2
mf
cresc.
decresc.
Ten 1
mf
cresc.
decresc.
Ten 2
mf
cresc.
decresc.
Bari
mf
cresc.
decresc.
F
Pno
mf
cresc.
decresc.
Bass
mf
cresc.
decresc.
Dr
33
"time" on hi-hat
cresc.
decresc.

Alt 1
Alt 2
Ten 1
Ten 2
Bari
Bass
Dr
Solo
cadenza
Solo
pp
pp
pp
pp
pp
f
mf
rit.
3
pp
38
G Calypso
solo (set tempo)
Alt 1
Alt 2
Ten 1
Ten 2
Bari
mf
G Calypso
Bass
Dr
mf
mf
43

6
Alt 1
Alt 2
Ten 1
Ten 2
Bari
Bass
Dr
Calypso
47
H
Alt 1
Alt 2
Ten 1
Ten 2
Bari
Bass
Dr
H
51
simile
Love and Smiles

Alt 1
Alt 2
Ten 1
Ten 2
Bari
Bass
Dr
55
I swing
Alt 1
Alt 2
Ten 1
Ten 2
Bari
I swing
Bass
swing
Dr
59

Alt 1
Alt 2
Ten 1
Ten 2
Bari
Bass
Dr
63
Alt 1
Alt 2
Ten 1
Ten 2
Bari
Bass
Dr
67
mf
mf
mf
f

J Calypso
Alt 1
mp
Alt 2
mp
Ten 1
mp
Ten 2
mp
Bari
J Calypso
Bass
mf
Dr
mf
71
Latin set-up
Alt 1
Alt 2
Ten 1
D
solo break
(1st soloist)*
Ten 2
Bari
Bass
(Calypso)
Dr
75
* On the recording Tenor Sax 1 took the first solo.
Love and Smiles

Love and Smiles

Alt 1
Alt 2
Ten 1
Ten 2
Bari
Bass
Dr
solo
solo
114
Alt 1
Alt 2
Ten 1
Ten 2
Bari
Bass
Dr
solo
solo
118
Love and Smiles

12
Alt 1
Alt 2
Ten 1
Ten 2
Bari
Bass
Dr
122
solo
solo
O
P
12
12
8
8
Alt 1
Alt 2
Ten 1
Ten 2
Bari
O
P
Bass
Dr
12
12
8
8
126
Love and Smiles

2
Q
Saxes (a cappella)
Alt 1
mp
Alt 2
mp
Ten 1
mp
Ten 2
mp
Bari
mp
2
Q
Saxes (a cappella)
Bass
Dr
128
Alt 1
Alt 2
Ten 1
Ten 2
Bari
Bass
Dr
132

Alt 1
Alt 2
Ten 1
Ten 2
Bari
Bass
Dr
cresc.
cresc.
cresc.
cresc.
cresc.
136
decresc.
decresc.
decresc.
decresc.
decresc.
f
f
f
f
f
mp
mp
mp
mp
pp
cresc.
mf
140

Alt 1
Alt 2
Ten 1
Ten 2
Bari
Bass
Dr
swing
mf
R
144
148
Love and Smiles

Alt 1
Alt 2
Ten 1
Ten 2
Bari
Bass
Dr
152
S Calypso
Alt 1
mp
Alt 2
mp
Ten 1
mp
Ten 2
mp
Bari
S Calypso
Bass
mf
Dr
156
Latin set-up

Alt 1
Alt 2
Ten 1
Ten 2
Bari
Bass
Dr
(Calypso)
160
T swing
mf
mf
mf
mf
mf
p
p
p
p
p
mf
mf
mf
mf
mf
mp
mp
mp
mp
mp
T swing
(mf)
"time" on hi-hat
mf
163
Love and Smiles

Alt 1
Alt 2
Ten 1
Ten 2
Bari
Bass
Dr
"time" on ride
mp
mp
simile
167
Alt 1
Alt 2
Ten 1
Ten 2
Bari
Bass
Dr
171

Alt 1
Alt 2
Ten 1
Ten 2
Bari
Bass
Dr
175
V
Alt 1
mf
cresc.
decresc.
Alt 2
mf
cresc.
decresc.
Ten 1
mf
cresc.
decresc.
Ten 2
mf
cresc.
decresc.
Bari
mf
cresc.
decresc.
V
Pno
mf
cresc.
decresc.
Bass
mf
cresc.
decresc.
Dr
181
"time" on hi-hat
cresc.
decresc.
Love and Smiles

Alt 1
Alt 2
Ten 1
Ten 2
Bari
Bass
Dr
Solo
mf
rit. 3
pp
pp
pp
pp
pp
pp
186
W
Solo
cadenza
slowly
mf
Alt 1
Bass
arco
Solo
mf
190

Love And Smiles

G
Calypso
solo (set tempo)
mf
43
47
H
51
55
p
I
swing
mf
59
63
67
J
Calypso
mp
71
75
^ A
4
solo break (1st soloist)

67
J Calypso
71
mp
75
solo break
(1st soloist)
A
4
K Solos Calypso
A   E/G#   F#m   F#m7   D   A/C#   Bm7   E7sus
80
Piano comps
A   E/G#   F#m   F#m7   D   A/C#   1. Bm7   E7sus   2. B7   E7   A6   A7   Dmaj7
84
L swing
(Dmaj7)   D#m7   G#7   Em7   Fdim7   F#m7   Gmaj7   G#m7b5   C#7(b9)
89
Bass walks
F#m   F#m(maj7)   F#m7   D#m7b5   D7   C#m7   F#7
93
Bm   Bm(maj7)   Bm7   G#m7b5   C#7   F#7   B7   E7
97
transition to Calypso
M Calypso
A   E/G#   F#m   F#m7   D   A/C#   Bm7   E7sus
101
A   E/G#   F#m   F#m7   D   A/C#   1. solos continue   back to K   2. last time   to I
B7   E7   A6   E7   B7   E7   A6
Piano
105
mp

ALTO SAX 2 (2nd part) page 3 - Love And Smiles
1 Drum chorus
N
mp
110
116
122
O
12
P
8
126
2 Saxes (a cappella)
Q
mp
128
132
cresc.
136
decresc.
f
140
mp
R swing
mf
144

Love And Smiles

ALTO SAX 2 (2nd part)

JERRY DODGION

67
J Calypso
mp
71
75
solo break
(1st soloist)
D
4
K Solos Calypso
D
A/C#
Bm
Bm7
G
D/F#
Em7
A7sus
Piano comps
80
D
A/C#
Bm
Bm7
G
D/F#
1.
Em7
A7sus
2.
E7 A7 D6 D7 Gmaj7
84
L swing
(Gmaj7)
G#m7 C#7
Am7
Bbdim7
Bm7
Cmaj7
C#m7b5
F#7(b9)
Bass walks
89
Bm
Bm(maj7)
Bm7
G#m7b5 G7
F#m7
B7
93
Em
Em(maj7)
Em7
C#m7b5
F#7
B7
E7
A7
transition to Calypso
97
M Calypso
D
A/C#
Bm
Bm7
G
D/F#
Em7
A7sus
101
D
A/C#
Bm
Bm7
G
D/F#
1. solos continue   back to K
E7   A7   D6   A7
2. last time   to I
E7   A7   D6
Piano
105
mp

Drum chorus
Saxes (a cappella)
mp
cresc.
decresc.
f
mp
swing
mf

Calypso
mp
156
160
swing
mf
p
mf
mp
163
167
171
175
cresc.
decresc.
mf
181
186
pp
4

Recorded on THE JOY OF SAX / Jerry Dodgion (Love and Smiles Music LSM 101)
TENOR SAX 1 (3rd part)
Love And Smiles
JERRY DODGION 
rubato
slow tempo (♩ = ca. 60)
faster (swing ♩ = ca. 90)
Alto 1 cue
solo Alto Sax 1
add Bass
cresc.
decresc.
Alto 1 cadenza
Calypso
Alto 1 sets tempo
swing
engraved by Osho Endo
Copyright © 1990, 2003 SECOND FLOOR MUSIC
International Copyright Secured   All Rights Reserved   Made in U.S.A.

TENOR SAX 2 (4th part) page 2 - Love And Smiles
67
J Calypso
71
mp
mf
75
^ D
4
solo break
(1st soloist)
K Solos Calypso
D   A/C#   Bm   Bm7   G   D/F#   Em7   A7sus
80
Piano comps
D   A/C#   Bm   Bm7   G   D/F#   1. Em7   A7sus   2. E7   A7 D6   D7 Gmaj7
84
L swing
(Gmaj7)   G#m7 C#7   Am7   Bbdim7   Bm7   Cmaj7   C#m7b5   F#7(b9)
89
Bass walks
Bm   Bm(maj7)   Bm7   G#m7b5 G7   F#m7   B7
93
Em   Em(maj7)   Em7   C#m7b5   F#7   B7   E7   A7
97
transition to Calypso
M Calypso
D   A/C#   Bm   Bm7   G   D/F#   Em7   A7sus
101
1. solos continue   back to K   2. last time   to I
D   A/C#   Bm   Bm7   G   D/F#   E7   A7 D6   A7   E7   A7 D6   Piano
105
mp

TENOR SAX 2 (4th part) page 3 - Love And Smiles
1 Drum chorus
N
110
mp
116
122
O
12
P
8
126
2 Saxes (a cappella)
Q
128
mp
132
136
cresc.
3
140
decresc.
f
mp
R swing
144
mf
3
3
3

TENOR SAX 2 (4th part) page 4 - Love And Smiles
S Calypso
T swing
U
V
W

Recorded on *THE JOY OF SAX* / *Jerry Dodgion* (*Love and Smiles Music LSM 101*)

TENOR SAX 2 (4th part)

Love And Smiles

JERRY DODGION

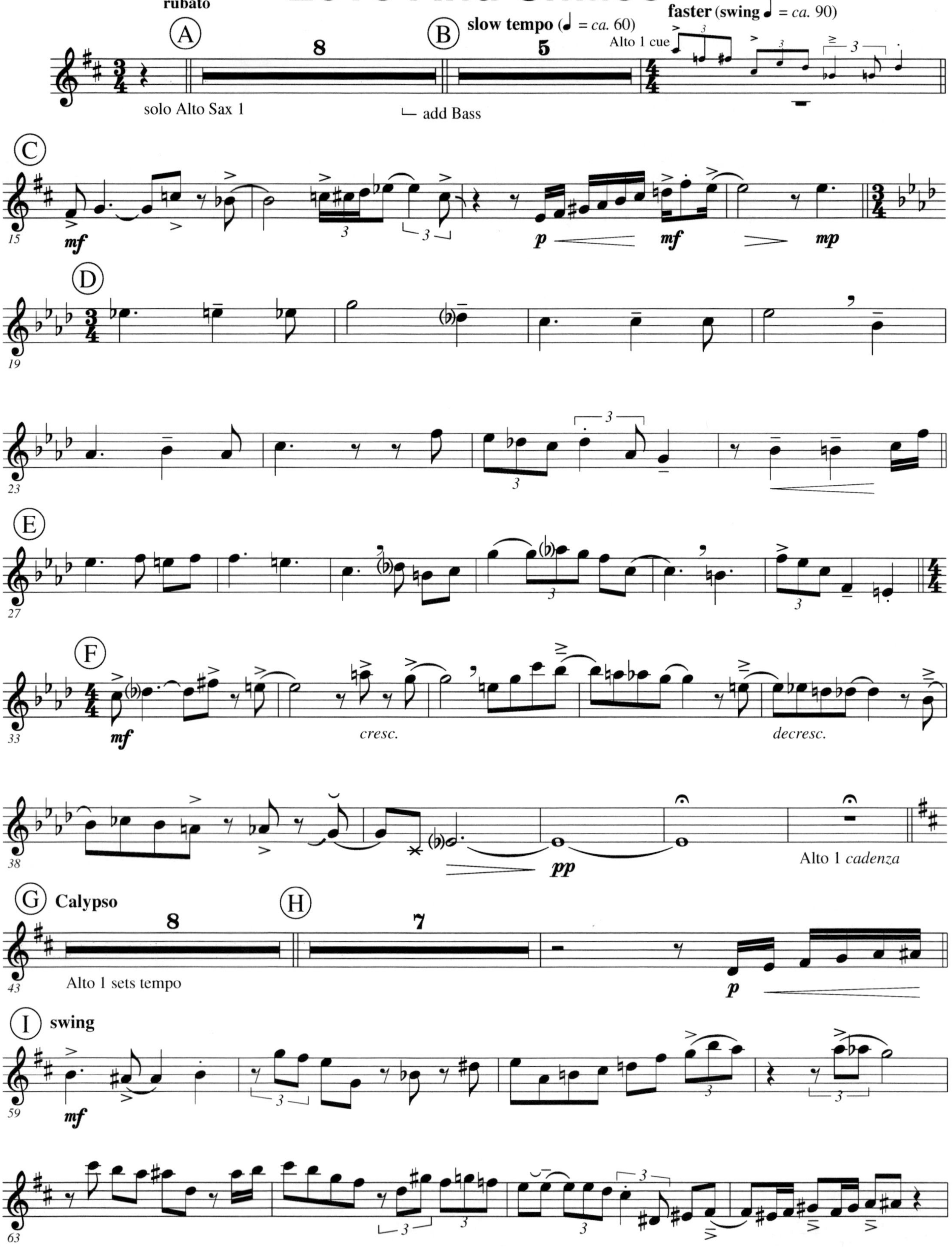

rubato
A
8
B
slow tempo (♩ = ca. 60)
5
faster (swing ♩ = ca. 90)
Alto 1 cue
solo Alto Sax 1
add Bass
C
15
mf
p
mf
mp
D
19
23
E
27
F
33
mf
cresc.
decresc.
38
pp
Alto 1 cadenza
G
Calypso
8
H
7
43
Alto 1 sets tempo
p
I
swing
59
mf
63

engraved by Osho Endo

Calypso
K Solos
C   G/B   Am   Am7   F   C/E   Dm7   G7sus
80   Piano comps
C   G/B   Am   Am7   F   C/E
1. Dm7   G7sus
2. D7   G7 C6   C7   Fmaj7
84
L swing
(Fmaj7)   F#m7 B7   Gm7   G#dim7   Am7   Bbmaj7   Bm7b5   E7(b9)
89   Bass walks
Am   Am(maj7)   Am7   F#m7b5 F7   Em7   A7
93
Dm   Dm(maj7)   Dm7   Bm7b5   E7   A7   D7   G7
97   transition to Calypso
M Calypso
C   G/B   Am   Am7   F   C/E   Dm7   G7sus
101
C   G/B   Am   Am7   F   C/E
1. solos continue   back to K
D7   G7   C6   G7
2. last time   to 1
D7   G7   C6   Piano
105
1 Drum chorus
N
mp
110
116
122
O 12   P 8
2 Saxes (a cappella)
Q
8   8
128

Calypso
G
mf
Alto 1 sets tempo
mf
H
I swing
J Calypso
mf
mf
solo break
(1st soloist)

Recorded on THE JOY OF SAX / Jerry Dodgion (Love and Smiles Music LSM 101)
Love And Smiles
BASS
JERRY DODGION
Solo Alto Sax 1
mf
play
mf
slow tempo (♩ = ca. 60)
faster (swing ♩ = ca. 90)
Alto 1 cue
(mf)
mp
cresc.
decresc.
mf
Solo
mf
rit.
Alto 1 cadenza
engraved by Osho Endo
Copyright © 1990, 2003 SECOND FLOOR MUSIC
International Copyright Secured   All Rights Reserved   Made in U.S.A.

Recorded on THE JOY OF SAX / Jerry Dodgion (Love and Smiles Music LSM 101)
BARITONE SAX (5th part)
Love And Smiles
JERRY DODGION
rubato
slow tempo (♩ = ca. 60)
faster (swing ♩ = ca. 90)
Alto 1 cue
solo Alto Sax 1
add Bass
mf
p
mf
mp
Calypso
Alto 1 sets tempo
Alto 1 cadenza
swing
mf
cresc.
decresc.
pp
mf
Copyright © 1990, 2003 SECOND FLOOR MUSIC
International Copyright Secured   All Rights Reserved   Made in U.S.A.
engraved by Osho Endo

148
152
mf
f
S Calypso
156
160
T swing
163
mf
p
mf
mp
U
167
171
175
V
181
mf
cresc.
decresc.
186
pp
W
4
3/4
4/4

BARITONE SAX (5th part) page 3 - Love And Smiles
1 Drum chorus
N
110
mp
116
122
O
P
12
8
126
2 Saxes (a cappella)
Q
128
mp
132
136
cresc.
140
decresc.
f
R swing
144
mf

67
J Calypso
71
75
solo break
(1st soloist)
A
4
Solos Calypso
K
A
E/G#
F#m
F#m7
D
A/C#
Bm7
E7sus
Piano comps
80
A
E/G#
F#m
F#m7
D
A/C#
1.
Bm7
E7sus
2.
B7 E7 A6
A7 Dmaj7
84
L swing
(Dmaj7)
D#m7 G#7
Em7
Fdim7
F#m7
Gmaj7
G#m7b5
C#7(b9)
Bass walks
89
F#m
F#m(maj7)
F#m7
D#m7b5 D7
C#m7
F#7
93
Bm
Bm(maj7)
Bm7
G#m7b5
C#7
F#7
B7
E7
transition to Calypso
97
M Calypso
A
E/G#
F#m
F#m7
D
A/C#
Bm7
E7sus
101
A
E/G#
F#m
F#m7
D
A/C#
1. solos continue   back to K
B7 E7 A6
E7
2. last time
to I
B7 E7 A6
Piano
105
mp

Love And Smiles

Dm
Dm(maj7)
Dm7
Bm7♭5
E7
A7
D7
G7
97
transition to Calypso
M Calypso
C
G/B
Am
Am7
F
C/E
Dm7
G7sus
101
C
G/B
Am
Am7
F
C/E
1. solos continue
back to K
D7
G7
C6
G7
2. last time
to 1
D7
G7
C6
Piano
mp
105
1 Drum chorus
N
8
8
O
12
P
8
110
2 Saxes (a cappella)
Q
8
8
R swing
12
S Calypso
7
128
T swing
4
U
8
6
163
V
mf
cresc.
decresc.
3
181
3
W
4
186

Recorded on THE JOY OF SAX / Jerry Dodgion (Love and Smiles Music LSM 101)
DRUMS
Love And Smiles
JERRY DODGION
rubato 
A
slow tempo (= ca. 60)
B
faster (swing = ca. 90)
Alto 1 cue
8
5
solo Alto Sax 1
add Bass
C
"time" on hi-hat
mf
D
"time" on ride
mp
simile
E
F
"time" on hi-hat
cresc.
Bass cue
rit.
decresc.
pp
Alto 1
cadenza
Calypso
G
mf
Alto 1 sets tempo
mf
(Calypso)
H
simile
Copyright © 1990, 2003 SECOND FLOOR MUSIC
International Copyright Secured   All Rights Reserved   Made in U.S.A.
engraved by Osho Endo

152
S Calypso
3
mf
Latin set-up
(Calypso)
160
T swing
"time" on hi-hat
3
3
163 mf
U "time" on ride
3/4
167 mp
simile
3
171
175
4/4
V
4/4
181 "time" on hi-hat
cresc.
decresc.
Bass cue
rit.
3
W
4
186
pp

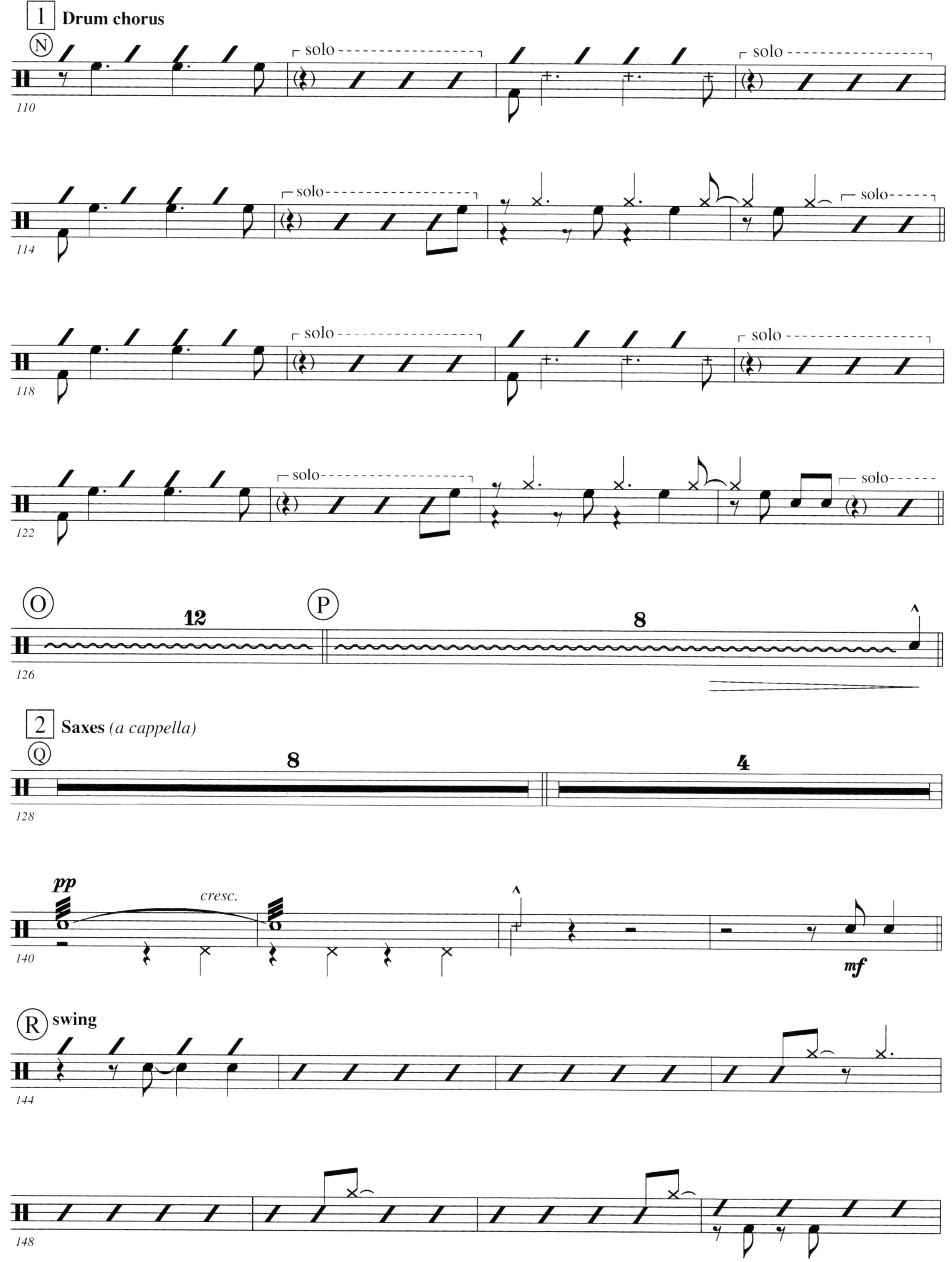
Drum chorus
solo
solo
solo
solo
solo
solo
solo
Saxes (a cappella)
cresc.
swing
pp
mf

55
I swing
59
63
67
J Calypso
3
mf
71
Latin set-up
(Calypso)
4
75
solo break
(1st soloist)
Calypso
K Solos
7
1.
2.
80
Piano comps
L swing
11
89
Bass walks
transition to Calypso
M Calypso
7
1. solos continue   back to K
2. last time   to 1
101
Piano
mp

Calypso
Solos
K
A
E/G#
F#m
F#m7
D
A/C#
Bm7
E7sus
Piano comps
80
A
E/G#
F#m
F#m7
D
A/C#
1.
Bm7
E7sus
2.
B7
E7 A6
A7 Dmaj7
84
L swing
(Dmaj7)
D#m7 G#7
Em7
Fdim7
F#m7
Gmaj7
G#m7b5
C#7(b9)
Bass walks
89
F#m
F#m(maj7)
F#m7
D#m7b5 D7
C#m7
F#7
93
Bm
Bm(maj7)
Bm7
G#m7b5
C#7
F#7
B7
E7
transition to Calypso
97
M Calypso
A
E/G#
F#m
F#m7
D
A/C#
Bm7
E7sus
101
A
E/G#
F#m
F#m7
D
A/C#
1. solos continue   back to K
B7
E7 A6
E7
2. last time   to 1
B7
E7 A6
Piano
105
1 Drum chorus
N
mp
110
mp
116

122
O
12
P
8
126
2
Saxes (a cappella)
Q
128
mp
132
136
cresc.
140
decresc.
f
mp
R
swing
144
mf
3
148
3
3
3
152
3

S Calypso
156
mp
160
T swing
163
mf
p mf mp
U 3/4
167
171
175
V 4/4
181
mf
cresc.
decresc.
186
pp
W Solo
cadenza slowly
190
mf
Bass